CELTIC
QUICK-FIX

Learn the Celtic Languages Quickly

Stephen Owen Rule

Cyflwynir y llyfr hwn i'm mab, Bedwyr Llŷr.
Gobeithio cawn siarad yr ieithoedd hyn gyda'n gilydd yn y dyfodol.

Scríobhtar an leabhar seo do mo mhac, Bedwyr Llŷr.
Tá súil agam go labhraíomid na teangacha seo le chéile sa tódhchaí.

Ta yn lioar shoh scruit er my vac, Bedwyr Llŷr.
Ta treisht orrym loayrmayd ny çhengaghyn shoh ry-cheilley 'sy traa ta ry-heet.

Tha an leabhar sin sgrìobhte airson mo mhac, Bedwyr Llŷr.
Tha mi an dòchas gum bruidhinn sinn na cànanan seo còmhla san àm ri teachd.

An lyver ma a skrifas dhe'm mab, Bedwyr Llŷr.
My a waytyas y bydhyn ow kewsel an yethow ma war-barth y'n termyn a dheu.

Skriver ul levr-mañ evit ma mab, Bedwyr Llŷr.
Emichañs e komzomp an yezhoù-mañ a-gevret en dazont.

MAP Y GWLEDYDD CELTAIDD /
MAP DE NA TÌORTHA CEILTEACHA /
CASLYS NY ÇHEERAGHYN CELTIAGH /
LÉARSCEÁIL NA TÌORTHA CEILTEACHA /
MAPPA AN GWLASOW KELTEK /
KARTENN AR BROIOÙ KELTIEK
(*Map of the Celtic Nations*) (Carte des Pays Celtiques)

Y GWLEDYDD CELTAIDD A'U HIEITHOEDD /
AN GWLASOW KELTEK HA'GA YETHOW /
NY ÇHEERAGHYN CELTIAGH AS NYN ÇHENGAGHYN /
NA DÙCHANNAN CEILTEACH AGUS NA CHÀNANAN ACU /
NA TÌORTHA CEILTEACHA AGUS A DTEANGACHA /
AR BROIOÙ KELTIEK HAG O YEZHOÙ

(*The Celtic Nations and their Languages*)
(Les Pays Celtiques et leurs Langues)

	Brezhoneg (Breton)	Cymraeg (Welsh)	Gaeilge (Irish)	Gàidhlig (Gaelic)	Gaelg (Manx)	Kernewek (Cornish)
Britanny Bretagne	Breizh	Llydaw	An Bhriotáin	A' Bhreatainn Bhig	Yn Vritaan	Breten Vian
Breton (language / langue)	Brezhoneg	Llydaweg	Briotáinis	Breatainnis	Britaanish	Bretonek
Cornwall	Kernev-Veur	Cernyw	An Chorn	A' Chòrn	Yn Chorn	Kernow
Cornish (language)	Kerneveurek	Cernyweg	An Choirnis	Còrnais	Cornish	Kernewek
Ireland	Iwerzhon	Iwerddon Ynys Werdd	Éire	Èirinn	Nerin	Iwerdhon Wordhon
Irish (language)	Iwerzhoneg	Gwyddeleg	Gaeilge	Gàidhlig na h-Èireann	Yernish	Iwerdhonek Wordhonek
(Isle of) Man(n)	Manav	(Ynys) Manaw	Oileán Mhanann	Eilean Mhanainn	Mannin Ellan Vannin	(Ynys) Manow
Manx (language)	Manaveg	Manaweg	Gaeilge Mhanann	Gàidhlig Mhanainn	Gaelg	Manowek
Scotland	Bro-Skos	Yr Alban	Albain	Alba	Nalbin	Alban
Gaelic (language)	Gouezeleg Skos	Gaeleg	Gaeilge na hAlban	Gàidhlig	Gaelg ny h-Albey	Albanek
Wales	Kembre	Cymru	Breatain Bheag	Cuimrigh A' Chuimrigh	Bretin	Kembra
Welsh (language)	Kembraeg	Cymraeg	Breatnais	Cuimris	Bretnish	Kembrek

RHAGAIR / FACAL-TOISICH / ROIE-RAA / RÉAMHRÁ / RAGLAVAR / RAKSKRID
(*Foreword*) (L'avant-propos)

As with any language the key to its vitality and to its survival lies in its use – no different can be said of the Celtic languages. Since compiling this book I have been more confident in using all six Celtic languages with greater proficiency on social networking sites like Twitter – *with the hope of giving the languages a new breath in the world of social media* – and in using the language verbally in conversation – *with the hope of setting free their wonderful sounds.*

If this book persuades just one person into swift acquisition of these ancient languages or, better still, into opening fully the doors of fluency in one or more of the languages, I shall rest happily.

It must be noted that the likelihood of making mistakes when creating sentences using this book will be high. My philosophy is to encourage living use of these languages in any and all formats without reservation or inhibition. Even so, the likelihood for understanding is equally as high. In addition, and from what I've come to learn of Celtic language speakers, the commendation for attempt and bravery will far outweigh any displeasure from language 'purists.' What these languages need more than anything is an opportunity to be seen, heard and used.

In addition to the linguistic acquisition offered by this book, it also provides ample opportunity to readily compare and contrast the numerous similarities between the six Celtic tongues that were first observed by Seòras Bochanan (George Buchanan) in 1582 and later (and more comprehensively) by Edward Lhuyd early in the 18th century – something which first caught my eye about these perculiar languages.

They say one should write a book according to what one would like to read. This is mine.

NODIADAU / NÓTAÍ / SCREEUYN / NOTAICHEAN / NOTYANSOW / NOTENNOÙ

(*Notes*) (Les Annotations)

- I have purposely left out large areas of each language with the hope that this starter guide will be enough of an incentive to further pursue each language.

- Tenses are provided in the first and third person singular only. This should provide adequate language for simple conversation and sentence building as well as opening doors for further study.

- Nouns are <u>not</u> included in this book because they can be found easily in their purest forms in various dictionaries or online lexicons. Be aware that all Celtic languages treat nouns (as well as some numbers and adjectives) as masculine and feminine.

- All verbs in the Celtic languages may be seen as 'to [verb]' OR '[verb]*ing*.' No change is made to the original verb unless otherwise stated.

- The meanings of prepositions vary from language to language giving rise to difficulties in translation. Sympathetic native speakers will, however, understand meanings despite perhaps them not being entirely grammatically correct in the target language. In addition, almost all prepositions in all Celtic languages conjugate when coupled with personal pronouns. Although not included in this book, they can be found readily in dictionaries, lexicons and online.

- Only Breton uses the indefinite article [Eng. *a / an*]. This is explained in the relevant chapter.

- All Celtic languages accommodate initial consonant mutation. The rules regarding these changes can be found in grammar books as well as online. The most common causes are explained throughout this book.

- Languages are arranged according to their native names in alphabetical (Latin) order except *Brezhoneg* (Breton) which appears in the last chapter and is trilingual with **Breton**, *English* and French.

CYNNWYS / CLÀR-INNSE / CUMMAL / CLÁR ÁBHAIR / SYNSAS / DONVEZIOÙ
(*Contents*) (Les Teneurs)

Each language section has been set out as follows;

TENSES; present, past [habitual and simple], conditional (via *I would like*) and future habitual and simple). There are also notes on mutations following each term.

VERBS; 18 common verbs have been translated into each language. Verbs in the Celtic languages conjugate but very few of them are shown here.

ADJECTIVES; 50 common adjectives have been translated into each language.

CONJUNCTIONS; 7 conjunctions are offered as well as their mutation effects on following words when applicable.

PREPOSITIONS; 7 prepositions are in each language as well as their mutation effects on following words when applicable. Prepositions in Celtic languages can become personalized; these are not shown in this book.

PLEASANTRIES AND IMPORTANT PHRASES; On the go or online... phrases important in any language.

NUMBERS; Numbers from 1 – 10. Mutations noted.

EXAMPLE TEXT; Article 1 of the Universal Declaration of Human Rights.

1. Cymraeg / Welsh

a. Amserau (*Tenses*)

b. Berfau (*Verbs*)

c. Ansoddeiriau (*Adjectives*)

d. Cysyllteiriau (*Conjunctions*)

e. Arddodiaid (*Prepositions*)

f. Ymadroddion (*Phrases*)

g. Rhifau (*Numbers*)

h. Testun Enghreifftiol (*Example Text*)

2. Gaeilge / Irish (Gaelic)

a. Amsirí (*Tenses*)

b. Briathra (*Verbs*)

c. Aidiachtaí (*Adjectives*)

d. Cónaisc (*Conjuctions*)

e. Réamhfhocail (*Prepositions*)

f. Frásaí (*Phrases*)

g. Uimhreacha (*Numbers*)

h. Téacs Samplach (*Example Text*)

3. Gaelg / Manx (Gaelic)

a. Emshiryn (*Tenses*)

b. Breearyn (*Verbs*)

c. Marennymyn (*Adjectives*)

d. Co-whingyssyn (*Conjunctions*)

e. Roie-ocklyn (*Prepositions*)

f. Abbyrtyn (*Phrases*)

g. Earrooyn (*Numbers*)

h. Teks Sambyl (*Example Text*)

4. Gàidhlig / (Scottish) Gaelic

a. Aimsirean (*Tenses*)

b. Gnìobhairean (*Verbs*)

c. Buadhairean (*Adjectives*)

d. Naisgearan (*Conjunctions*)

e. Riomhearan (*Prepositions*)

f. Abairtean (*Phrases*)

g. Uibhirean (*Numbers*)

h. Teacsa Sampaill (*Example Text*)

5. Kernewek / Cornish

1. Amseryow (*Tenses*)

2. Verbow (*Verbs*)

3. Henwyn Gwann (*Adjectives*)

4. Geryow Kevrenn (*Conjunctions*)

5. Rageryow (*Prepositions*)

6. Lavarow (*Phrases*)

7. Niverow (*Numbers*)

8. Tekst Sempel (*Example Text*)

6. Brezhoneg / Breton

a. Amzeroù (*Tenses*)

b. Verboù (*Verbs*)

c. Anvioù-gwan (*Adjectives*)

d. Stagelloù (*Conjunctions*)

e. Araogennoù (*Prepositions*)

f. Rannfrazennoù (*Phrases*)

g. Niverennoù (*Numbers*)

h. Testen Skouer (*Example Text*)

1. CYMRAEG (*Welsh*)

a. AMSERAU (*Tenses*)

- Both **o** and **e** are used to convey *he* in northern and southern Welsh respectively. The literary term is **ef**.
- Terms beginning with **W**s are often omitted in speech and are occastionally omitted in writing.

Dw i'n	*I am / I do*
Dw i ddim yn	*I am not / I don't*
Mae o'n/e'n	*He is / He does*
Dydy o/e ddim yn	*He isn't / He doesn't*
Mae hi'n	*She is / She does*
Dydy hi ddim yn	*She isn't / She doesn't*
Mae ___ yn	*___ is / ___ does*
Dydy ___ ddim yn	*___ isn't / ___ doesn't*

Roeddwn i'n	*I was*
Doeddwn i ddim yn	*I wasn't*
Roedd o'n/e'n	*He was*
Doedd o/e ddim yn	*He wasn't*
Roedd hi'n	*She was*
Doedd hi ddim yn	*She wasn't*
Roedd ___ yn	*___ was*
Doedd ___ ddim yn	*___ wasn't*

Wnes i [SM]	*I did*
Wnes i ddim	*I didn't*
Wnaeth o/e [SM]	*He did*
Wnaeth o/e ddim	*He didn't*
Wnaeth hi [SM]	*She did*
Wnaeth hi ddim	*She didn't*
Wnaeth ___ [SM]	*___ did*
Wnaeth ___ ddim	*___ didn't*

Hoffwn i [SM]	*I would like (to)*
Hoffwn i ddim	*I wouldn't like (to)*
Hoffai o/e [SM]	*He would like (to)*
Hoffai o/e ddim	*He wouldn't like (to)*
Hoffai hi [SM]	*She would like (to)*
Hoffai hi ddim	*She wouldn't like (to)*
Hoffai ___ [SM]	*___ would like (to)*
Hoffai ___ ddim	*___ wouldn't like (to)*

Wna' i [SM]	*I will / I shall*
Wna' i ddim	*I will not / I shall not*
Wneith o/e [SM]	*He will / He shall*
Wneith o/e ddim	*He will not / He shall not*
Wneith hi [SM]	*She will / She shall*
Wneith hi ddim	*She will not / She shall not*
Wneith ___ [SM]	*___ will / ___ shall*
Wneith ___ ddim	*___ will not / ___ shall not*

Bydda i'n	*I will be*
Fydda i ddim yn	*I will not be*
Bydd o'n/e'n	*He will be*
Fydd o/e ddim yn	*He will not be*
Bydd hi'n	*She will be*
Fydd hi ddim yn	*She will not be*
Bydd ___ yn	*___ will be*
Fydd ___ ddim yn	*___ will not be*

b. BERFAU (*Verbs*)

- Putting **wedi** before verbs in Welsh denotes the perfect tense. The particle **yn** (and therefore **'n**) are not included where **wedi** is used.
- Tenses in section a. that do not include **yn** (and therefore **'n**) will cause a soft mutation on any word that follows. The negating **ddim** triggers no mutation.

mynd (i)	*to go (to)*	**deall / dallt**	*to understand*
cael	*to get (to)*	**ysgrifennu**	*to write*
cael	*to have (a)*	**darllen**	*to read*
cymryd	*to take*	**gwylio**	*to watch*
mwynhau	*to enjoy*	**dweud (wrth)**	*to tell (to)*
agor	*to open*	**siarad (â)**	*to talk / speak (to)*
cau	*to close*	**rhoi**	*to give / to put*
bwyta	*to eat*	**cysgu**	*to sleep*
yfed	*to drink*	**gwneud**	*to do / to make*
prynu	*to buy / purchase*	**bod**	*to be*
cerdded	*to walk*	**gwrando (ar)**	*to listen to*
rhedeg	*to run*	**meddwl**	*to think*
eistedd	*to sit [down]*	**credu (mewn)**	*to believe (in)*
sefyll	*to stand [up]*	**clywed**	*to hear*
gwisgo	*to wear*	**caru**	*to love*
edrych (ar)	*to look (at)*	**dysgu**	*to learn*
gweld	*to see*	**chwarae (dros)**	*to play (for)*
dweud	*to say*	**gweithio (i)**	*to work (for)*

Y TREIGLAD MEDDAL [SM] (*The Soft Mutation*)

P	T	C	B	D	G	M	LL	RH
B	D	G	F	DD	-	F	L	R

NB: Adjectives beginning with **LL** and **RH** that follow yn (/ **'n**) will not mutate – **yn** r̲had = *cheap(ly)*

c. ANSODDEIRIAU (*Adjectives*)

- Adjectives (in most cases) follow the noun in Welsh. Words such as **hen** (*old*) come before nouns and cause a soft mutation on said noun: **hen wlad** = *(an) old country*. These, however, are rare and are found mainly in poetic language.
- Adverbs are formed by placing **yn** before the adjective and adding a soft mutation ∴ **yn fawr** = *largely*.

bad	**drwg**	*interesting*	**diddorol**
beautiful	**hardd, prydferth**	*important*	**pwysig**
big, large	**mawr**	*little*	**bach**
boring	**diflas**	*long*	**hir**
busy	**prysur**	*mean, nasty*	**cas**
cheap	**rhad**	*near*	**agos, clòs**
cold	**oer**	*new*	**newydd**
correct	**cywir**	*next*	**nesaf**
dangerous	**peryglus**	*old*	**hen**
different	**gwahanol**	*pretty*	**del, pert**
difficult	**anodd**	*right (fine, ok)*	**iawn**
dry	**sych**	*sad*	**trist**
easy, simple	**hawdd, rhwydd**	*short*	**byr**
excellent	**ardderchog**	*slow*	**araf**
expensive	**drud**	*small*	**bach, bychan**
false, fake	**ffug**	*soft*	**meddal**
fast, quick	**cyflym**	*special*	**arbennig**
fine	**braf, iawn**	*sure*	**sicr, siŵr**
full	**llawn**	*tall*	**tal**
good	**da**	*tired*	**blinedig**
happy	**hapus**	*true*	**gwir**
hard	**caled**	*ugly*	**hyll**
hot	**poeth**	*wet*	**gwlyb**
incorrect	**anghywir**	*young*	**ifanc**

d. CYSYLLTEIRIAU (*Conjunctions*)

a[AM] (ac before a vowel)	*and*
ond	*but / however*
neu[SM]	*or*
eto	*yet / again*
felly	*so / therefore*
hefyd	*too / also*
weithiau	*sometimes*
achos, oherwydd	*because*

e. ARDDODIAID (*Prepositions*)

am[SM]	*about, at (a time)*
ar[SM]	*on*
at[SM]	*at, to(wards)*
gan[SM]	*by, with*
heb[SM]	*without*
i[SM]	*to, for*
o[SM]	*of, from*
yn[NM], mewn	*in, in a*

Y TREIGLAD TRWYNOL [NM] (*The Nasal Mutation*)

P	MH
T	NH
C	NGH
B	M
D	N
G	NG

Y TREIGLAD LLAES [AM] (*The Aspirate Mutation*)

P	PH
T	TH
C	CH

fi	*me*	fy [NM]	*my*
ti	*you*	dy [SM]	*your*
fo	*he / him*	ei [SM]	*his*
hi	*she / her*	ei [AM (+H)]	*her*
ni	*we / us*	ein [(+H)]	*our*
chi	*you (pl.)*	eich	*your (pl.)*
nhw	*they / them*	eu [(+H)]	*their*

SM = Soft Mutation
NM = Nasal Mutation
AM = Aspirate Mutation
+H = Add **H** to words
beginning with vowels
(= A, E, I, O, U, W & Y)

f. YMADRODDION (*Phrases*)

Bore da	*Good morning*
P'nawn da	*Good afternoon*
Noswaith dda	*Good evening*
Nos da	*Good night*
Sut wyt ti?	*How are you? (Informal)*
Sut 'dych chi?	*How are you? (Formal)*
S'mai / Shw'mae	*Hi / Hello*
Ti'n iawn?	*(Are) you alright?*
Iechyd da	*Cheers / Good health*
Hwyl fawr / Da bo (chi)	*Goodbye*
Os gwelwch yn dda / Plîs	*Please*
Diolch (yn fawr (iawn))	*Thank you (very much)*
Esgusodwch fi	*Excuse me*

Mae gen' i [SM] **/ Mae (gy)da fi** [SM]	*I have [got] (a)*
Dw i eisiau / mo'yn	*I want (a / to)*
Dw i angen	*I need (a / to)*
Dw i heb [SM]	*I don't have / I'm yet to [lit. I'm without]*
Dw i methu	*I cannot [lit. I am failing (to)]*
Dw i ddim yn deall (hynny)	*I don't understand (that)*
Dw i'n dysgu Cymraeg	*I'm learning Welsh*

Cymru am byth	*Wales forever*

g. RHIFAU (*Numbers*)

Number	Cymraeg *masc. / fem.*
1	Un / Un [SM]
2	Dau [SM] / Dwy [SM]
3	Tri [AM] / Tair
4	Pedwar / Pedair
5	Pump (sometimes Pum [NM])
6	Chwech & (sometimes Chwe [AM])
7	Saith
8	Wyth
9	Naw
10	Deg (sometimes Deng [NM])

h. TESTUN ENGHREIFFTIOL (*Example Text*)

Genir pawb yn rhydd ac yn gydradd â'i gilydd mewn urddas a hawliau. Fe'u cynysgaeddir â rheswm a chydwybod, a dylai pawb ymddwyn y naill at y llall mewn ysbryd cymodlon.

All human beings are born free and equal in dignity and rights. They are endowed with reason and conscience and should act towards one another in a spirit of brotherhood.

2. GAEILGE (*Irish Gaelic*)

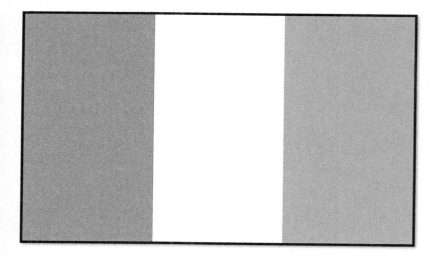

a. AIMSIRÍ (*Tenses*)

Tá mé	*I am / I do*
Níl mé	*I'm not / I don't*
Tá sé	*He is / He does*
Níl sé	*He isn't / He doesn't*
Tá sí	*She is / She does*
Níl sí	*She isn't / She doesn't*
Tá ___	*___ is / ___ doesn*
Níl ___	*___ isn't / ___ doesn't*

Verbs following the above affix **ag** *before them:* **Tá mé <u>ag</u> ithe** = *I am [at] eating / I do eat. No such additions occur when using adjectives.*

Bhí mé	*I was / I used to*
Ní raibh mé	*I wasn't / I didn't used to*
Bhí sé	*He was / He used to*
Ní raibh sé	*He wasn't / He didn't used to*
Bhí sí	*She was / She used to*
Ní raibh sí	*She wasn't / She didn't used to*
Bhí ___	*___ was / ___ used to*
Ní raibh ___	*___ wasn't / ___ used to*

Verbs following the above affix **ag** *before them:* **Bhí mé <u>ag</u> foghlaim** = *I was / used to be [at] learning. No such additions occur when using adjectives.*

Rinne mé	*I did*
Ní rinne mé	*I didn't*
Rinne sé	*He did*
Ní rinne sé	*He didn't*
Rinne sí	*She did*
Ní rinne sí	*She didn't*
Rinne ___	*___ did*
Ní rinne ___	*___ didn't*

> ⊰ Unlike Manx, Irish never uses 'rinne' (≈ 'done', 'made') as an auxiliary verb into the past tense. Instead, there is an initial lenition on infinitive verb and the pronoun follows; **dhún mé an doras** = *I closed the door.*

Ba mhaith liom	*I would like (to)*
Ní ba mhaith liom	*I wouldn't like (to)*
Ba mhaith leis	*He would like (to)*
Ní ba mhaith leis	*He wouldn't like (to)*
Ba mhaith léi	*She would like (to)*
Ní ba mhaith léi	*She wouldn't like (to)*
Ba mhaith le ___	*___ would like (to)*
Ní mhaith le ___	*___ wouldn't like (to)*

Déanfaidh mé	*I will do, make*	◅ The future tense in Irish is made by adding the suffix **-f(a)idh** to the end of a verbal noun.
Ní dhéanfaidh mé	*I will not do, make*	
Déanfaidh sé	*He will /do, make*	
Ní dhéanfaidh sé	*He will not do, make*	The irregular verb *'to do / make'* has been used in its future tense form to show how the suffix is applied.
Déanfaidh sí	*She will do, make*	
Ní dhéanfaidh sí	*She will not do, make*	
Déanfaidh ___	*___ will do, make*	NB The examples here are never used as an auxiliary verb like the other Celtic languages.
Ní dhéanfaidh ___	*___ will not do, make*	

Beidh mé	*I will (be)*
Ní bheidh mé	*I will not (be)*
Beidh sé	*He will (be)*
Ní bheidh sé	*He will not (be)*
Beidh sí	*She will (be)*
Ní bheidh sí	*She will not (be)*
Beidh ___	*___ will (be)*
Ní bheidh ___	*___ will not (be)*

Verbs following the above affix **ag** *before them:* **Beidh mé <u>ag</u> caint** = *I will speak / I will be [at] speaking. No such additions occur when using adjectives.*

b. BRIATHRA (*Verbs*)

- As alluded to in section a., the particle **ag** is added before the following and after the terms in section a. which are noted.
- On many occasions, Irish places a lenited form of a verb at the end of a clause; **Ba mhaith liom obair a <u>dhéanamh</u>** = *I'd like to <u>do</u> work.*
- Putting **tar éis** or **i ndiaidh** before verbs in Irish denotes the perfect tense. This form largely employs the form described in the previous point.

dul (go)	*to go (to)*	**tuiscint**	*to understand*
fáil	*to get [a]*	**scríobh**	*to write*
fáil	*to have [a]*	**léamh**	*to read*
tógáil	*to take*	**féachaint (ar)**	*to watch*
bain taitneamh as	*to enjoy*	**insint**	*to tell*
iarraidh	*to want (to)*	**labhairt (le)**	*to talk / speak (to)*
dúnadh	*to close*	**tabhairt**	*to give / put*
ithe	*to eat*	**codladh**	*to sleep*
ól	*to drink*	**déanamh**	*to do / make*
ceannach	*to buy / purchase*	**bheith**	*to be*
siúl	*to walk*	**éisteacht (le)**	*to listen (to)*
rith	*to run*	**smaoineamh**	*to think*
suí	*to sit*	**creidiúint**	*to believe*
seasamh	*to stand*	**cloisteáil**	*to hear*
caitheamh	*to wear*	**grá**	*to love*
breathnú (ar)	*to look (at)*	**foghlaim**	*to learn*
féach ar	*to see*	**imirt**	*to play*
rá	*to say*	**obair**	*to work*

SÉIMHIÚ (*Lenition*)

B	C	D	F	G	M	P	S	T
BH	CH	DH	FH	GH	MH	PH	SH	TH

Notes on pronunciation & when the **séimhiú** happens can be found readily in grammar books & online.

---

c. AIDIACHTAÍ (*Adjectives*)

- Adding the particle **go** (**go h-** before a vowel) before the adjective equates to the adverbial form.
- All Celtic languages can pluralise adjectives, but none stick to the rules quite as much as Irish. The general rule of thumb is to add an **-a** to the end.

bad	**dona**	*interesting*	**suimiúil**
beautiful	**álainn**	*important*	**tábhachtach**
big, large	**mór**	*little*	**beag**
boring	**leadránach**	*long*	**fada**
busy	**gnóthach**	*nasty, evil*	**olc**
cheap	**saor / suarach**	*near (to)*	**in aice (le)**
cold	**fuair**	*new*	**nua, úr**
correct	**ceart**	*next*	**seo chugainn**
dangerous	**contúirteacha**	*old*	**sean**
different	**difriúil**	*pretty*	**deas**
difficult	**deacair**	*right (= fine, ok)*	**ceart**
dry	**tirim**	*sad*	**brónach**
easy, simple	**éasca**	*short*	**gearr**
excellent	**iontach**	*slow*	**mall**
expensive	**daor**	*small*	**beag**
false, incorrect	**mícheart, cearr**	*soft*	**bog**
fast, quick	**luath**	*special*	**speisialta**
fine	**breá**	*sure, certain*	**cinnte**
full	**lán**	*tall*	**ard**
good	**maith**	*tired*	**tuirseach**
happy	**sásta, sona**	*true*	**fíor**
hard	**crua**	*ugly*	**gránna**
hot	**te**	*wet*	**fliuch**
huge	**ollmhór**	*young*	**óg**

d. CÓNAISC (Conjunctions)

agus	*and*
ach	*but*
nó	*or*
arís	*again*
mar sin	*so, therefore*
freisin, chomh maith	*too, also*
uaireanta	*sometimes*
mar	*because*

e. RÉAMHFHOCAIL (Prepositions)

ag	*at*
faoi	*about*
ar	*on*
go dtí	*to(wards)*
le	*by / with*
gan	*without*
do	*to / for*
ó	*of / from*
i(n)	*in*

URÚ NM (*Eclipsis*)

P	bP
T	dT
G	nG
F	bhF
E / I	n-E / n-I

mé	*me*	**mo** L	*my*
tú	*you*	**do** L	*your*
sé	*him*	**a** L	*his*
sí	*her*	**a** (+H)	*her*
muid	*us*	**ár** E (+N-)	*our*
sibh	*you (pl.)*	**bhur** E	*your (pl.)*
siad	*them*	**a** E (+N-)	*their*

L = Lenition

E = Eclipsis

+H / +N- = Add **H** or **N-**
to words beginning
with vowels

(= A, E, I, O & U)

f. FRÁSAÍ (*Phrases*)

Maidin mhaith	*Good morning*
Tráthnóna maith	*Good afternoon*
Tráthnóna maith	*Good evening*
Oíche mhaith	*Good night*
Conas atá tú? / Cen chaoí bhfuil tú?	*How are you? (Informal)*
Conas atá sibh? / Cen chaoí bhfuil sibh?	*How are you? (Formal)*
Dia duit / Dia dhaoibh	*Hi / Hello (Inf. / Form.)*
An bhfuil tú ceart (go leor)?	*(Are) you alright?*
Sláinte (mhaith)	*Cheers / Good health*
Slán (leat / anois)	*Goodbye*
Le do thoil / Le bhur dtoil	*Please (Inf. / Form.)*
Go raibh maith agat / GRM agaibh	*Thank you (Inf. / Form.)*
Gabh mo leithscéal	*Excuse me*

Tá ___ agam	*I have (got) (a)*
Tá ___ uaim	*I want (a / to)*
Is gá dom	*I need (a / to)*
Níl ___ agam	*I don't have*
Ní féidir liom	*I cannot*
Ní thigim (é sin)	*I don't understand (that)*
Tá mé ag foghlaim <u>Gaeilge</u>	*I'm learning <u>Irish</u>*
Foghlaimím <u>Gaeilge</u>	

<u>Éirinn</u> go bráth	*<u>Ireland</u> forever*

g. UIMHREACHA (*Numbers*)

Number	Gaeilge
1	a hAon
2	a Dó
3	a Trí
4	a Ceathair
5	a Cúig
6	a Sé
7	a Seacht
8	a hOcht
9	a Naoi
10	a Deich

h. TÉACS SAMPLACH (*Example Text*)

Saolaítear na daoine uile saor agus comhionann ina ndínit agus ina gcearta. Tá bua an réasúin agus an choinsiasa acu agus dlíd iad féin d'iompar de mheon bráithreachais i leith a chéile.

All human beings are born free and equal in dignity and rights. They are endowed with reason and conscience and should act towards one another in a spirit of brotherhood.

3. GAELG (*Manx Gaelic*)

a. EMSHIRYN (*Tenses*)

Ta mee	*I am / I do*
Cha nel mee	*I am not / I do not*
T'eh	*He / He is / He does*
Cha nel eh	*He isn't / He doesn't*
T'ee	*She / She is / She does*
Cha nel ee	*She isn't / She doesn't*
Ta ___	*___ / ___ is / ___ does*
Cha nel ___	*___ isn't / ___ doesn't*

Va mee	*I was*
Cha row mee	*I wasn't*
V'eh	*He was*
Cha row eh	*He wasn't*
V'ee	*She was*
Cha row ee	*She wasn't*
Va ___	*___ was*
Cha row ___	*___ wasn't*

Ren mee	*I did*
Cha ren mee	*I didn't*
Ren eh	*He did*
Cha ren eh	*He didn't*
Ren ee	*She did*
Cha ren ee	*She didn't*
Ren ___	*___ did*
Cha ren ___	*___ didn't*

◄ *The past tense can also be created in a similar fashion to how Irish and Gaelic form them; by leniting an infinitive and adding a personal pronoun. Unlike its two sister languages, Manx seems to prefer the* **'ren'** *formation.*

By vie lhiam	*I would like (to)*
Cha by vie lhiam	*I wouldn't like (to)*
By vie lesh	*He would like (to)*
Cha by vie lesh	*He wouldn't like (to)*
By vie lhee	*She would like (to)*
Cha by vie lhee	*She wouldn't like (to)*
By vie lesh ___	*___ would like (to)*
Cha by vie lesh ___	*___ wouldn't like (to)*

Neeym	*I will / I shall*
Cha jeanym	*I will not / I shall not*
Nee eh	*He will / He shall*
Cha jean eh	*He will not / He shall not*
Nee ish	*She will*
Cha jean ee	*She will not / She shall not*
Nee ___	*___ will / ___ shall*
Cha jean ___	*___ will not / ___ shall not*

Bee mee / Beeym	*I will (be)*
Cha bee mee / Cha beeym	*I will not (be)*
Bee eh	*He will (be)*
Cha bee eh	*He will not (be)*
Bee ish	*She will (be)*
Cha bee ish	*She will not (be)*
Bee ___	*___ will (be)*
Cha bee ___	*___ will not (be)*

b. BREEARYN (*Verbs*)

goll (dy)	*to go (to)*	**toiggal**	*to understand*
geddyn	*to get (to)*	**screeu**	*to write*
geddyn	*to have (a)*	**lhaih**	*to read*
goaill	*to take*	**jeeaghyn (er)**	*to watch*
goaill soylley	*to enjoy*	**loayrt (rish)**	*to tell (to)*
fosley	*to open*	**taggloo, caaynt**	*to talk, speak*
dooin	*to close*	**cur**	*to give / to put*
gee	*to eat*	**cadley**	*to sleep*
giu	*to drink*	**jannoo**	*to do / to make*
kionnaghey	*to buy, purchase*	**[dy] ve**	*to be*
shooyl	*to walk*	**eastiagh (rish)**	*to listen to*
roie	*to run*	**smooinaghey**	*to think*
soie	*to sit*	**credjal**	*to believe*
shassoo	*to stand*	**clashtyn**	*to hear*
ceau	*to wear*	**cur graih da**	*to love*
jeeaghyn (er)	*to look (at)*	**gynsagh**	*to learn*
fakin	*to see*	**cloie (rish)**	*to play (with)*
abbyr	*to say*	**gobbragh**	*to work*

BOGGAGHYS (*Lenition*)

P	T(H)	ÇH	C/K	QU	B	BW	D(H)	J/G	M
PH	H	H	CH	WH	V	W	GH	GH/Y	V

Notes on pronunciation & when the **boggaghys** happens can be found readily in grammar books & online.

c. MARENNYMYN (*Adjectives*)

- Derived adverbs are made by putting dy before the relevant adjective: **tappee** = *quick*, **dy tappee** = *quickly*.

bad	**drogh**	*interesting*	**symoil**
beautiful	**aalin**	*important*	**scanshoil**
big	**mooar**	*little*	**beg**
boring	**tiolley**	*long*	**liauyr**
busy	**tarroogh**	*nasty / evil*	**graney**
cheap	**neugheyr**	*near*	**faggys**
cold	**feayr**	*new*	**noa**
correct	**kiart**	*next*	**(by) niessey**
dangerous	**danjeyragh**	*old*	**shenn**
different	**anghasley**	*pretty*	**bwaagh**
difficult	**doillee**	*right / correct*	**kiart**
dry	**creeney**	*sad*	**trimshey**
easy / simple	**aashagh**	*short*	**giare**
excellent	**yindyssagh**	*slow*	**moal**
expensive	**deyr**	*small*	**beg**
false	**breagagh, foalsey**	*soft*	**bog**
fast / quick	**tappee**	*special*	**er lheh**
fine	**breaw**	*sure, certain*	**shickyr**
full	**lane**	*tall*	**ard**
good	**mie**	*tired*	**skee**
happy	**maynrey**	*true*	**feer**
hard	**creoi**	*ugly*	**graney**
hot	**çheh**	*wet*	**fliugh**
incorrect	**anchiart**	*young*	**aeg**

d. CO-WHINGYSSYN (*Conjunctions*)

as	*and*
agh	*but / however*
ny	*or*
reesh	*again*
myr shen	*so / therefore*
myrgheddyn	*too / also*
ny keartyn	*sometimes*
er yn oyr, er son	*because, for the sake of*

e. ROIE-OCKLYN (*Prepositions*)

mysh	*about*
er	*on*
ec	*at*
lesh	*by, with*
dyn [L], **gyn** [L]	*without*
da	*to, for*
dy, veih	*of, from*
ayns / sy	*in / in the*

STRONNAGHEY
(*Eclipsis*)

P	B
T(H)	D(H)
ÇH	J
C/K/Q	G
B	M
D(H)/J	N
G	NG
F	V
FW	W

L = Lenition

E = Eclipsis

N, **G** and **H** can be prefixed to words in various situations.

mee	*me*	**my** [L]	*my*
oo, ou	*you*	**dty** [L]	*your*
she	*him*	**e** [L]	*his*
shi	*her*	**e/y**	*her*
shin	*us*	**nyn** [E] (__ ain)	*our*
shiu	*you (pl.)*	**nyn** [E] (__ eu)	*your (pl.)*
ad	*them*	**nyn** [E] (__ oc)	*their*

f. ABBYRTYN (*Phrases*)

Moghrey mie	*Good morning*
Fastyr mie	*Good afternoon*
Fastyr mie	*Good evening*
Oie vie	*Good night*
Ky's t'ou?	*How are you? (Informal)*
Kanys ta shiu?	*How are you? (Formal)*
Hoi / Hello	*Hi / Hello (Inf. / Form.)*
Vel oo kiart (dy liooar)?	*(Are) you alright?*
Slaynt (vie)	*Cheers / Good health*
Slane (lesh / nish)	*Goodbye*
My sailt / My sailliu	*Please (Inf. / Form.)*
Gura mie ayd / Gura mie eu	*Thank you (Inf. / Form.)*
Gow my leshtal	*Excuse me*
Cha nel mee toiggal (eh shin)	*I don't understand (that)*
Ta _____ aym	*I have (got) (a)*
Ta mee laccal	*I want (a / to)*
S'lhiass dou	*I need (a / to)*
Cha nel _____ aym	*I don't have*
Cha noddym	*I cannot*
Ta mee gynsagh Gaelg	*I'm learning Manx*
Mannin (er son) dy bragh	*Isle of Man forever*

g. EARROOYN (*Numbers*)

Number	Gaelg
1	Un / Nane [L]
2	Jees / Daa [L]
3	Tree
4	Kiare
5	Queig
6	Shey
7	Shiaght
8	Hoght
9	Nuy
10	Jeih

h. TEKSYN SAMBYL (*Example Text*)

Ta dagh ooilley pheiagh ruggit seyr as corrym ayns ard-cheim as kiartyn. Ren jee feoiltaghey resoon as cooinsheanse orroo as by chair daue ymmyrkey ry cheilley myr braaraghyn.

All human beings are born free and equal in dignity and rights. They are endowed with reason and conscience and should act towards one another in a spirit of brotherhood.

4. **GÀIDHLIG** (*Scottish Gaelic*)

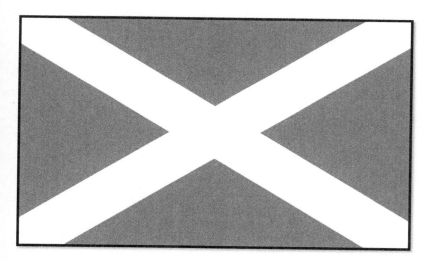

a. AIMSIREAN (*Tenses*)

Tha mi	*I am / I do*
Chan eil mi	*I am not / I don't*
Tha e	*He / He is / He does*
Chan eil e	*He isn't / He doesn't*
Tha i	*She / She is / She does*
Chan eil i	*She isn't / She doesn't*
Tha ___	*___ / ___is / ___does*
Chan eil ___	*___ isn't / ___ doesn't*

> *Verbs following the above affix* **a' / ag** *before them:* **Tha mi ag ithe** = *I am [at] eating / I do eat. No such additions occur when using adjectives.*

Bha mi	*I was*
Cha robh mi	*I wasn't*
Bha e	*He was*
Cha robh e	*He wasn't*
Bha i	She was
Cha robh i	*She wasn't*
Bha ___	*___ was*
Cha robh ___	*___ wasn't*

> *Verbs following the above affix* **a' / ag** *before them:* **Bha mi ag ionnsachadh** = *I was [at] learning. No such additions occur when using adjectives.*

Rinn mi	*I did*
Cha do rinn mi	*I didn't*
Rinn e	*He did*
Cha do rinn e	*He didn't*
Rinn i	*She did*
Cha do rinn i	*She didn't*
Rinn ___	*___ did*
Cha do rinn ___	*___ didn't*

> ◁ *Using 'rinn' as an auxiliary ver to create the past tense in Gaelic i rather crude and seldom done despite being widely understood The more common form is to lenit the first letter of an infinitive an add a personal pronoun;* **tuigsin** *(to understand) >* **thuig m** *(I understood).*

Bu toil leam / Bu toigh leam	*I would like (to)*
Cha bu toil leam	*I wouldn't like (to)*
Bu toil leis	*He would like (to)*
Cha bu toil leis	*He wouldn't like (to)*
Bu toil leatha	*She would like (to)*
Cha bu toil leatha	*She wouldn't like (to)*
Bu toil le ___	*___ would like (to)*
Cha bu toil le ___	*___ wouldn't like (to)*

Nì mi	*I will do, make*
Cha dèan mi	*I will not do, make*
Nì e	*He will do, make*
Cha dèan e	*He will not do, make*
Nì i	*She will do, make*
Cha dèan i	*She will not do, make*
Nì ___	*___ will do, make*
Cha dèan ___	*___ will not do, make*

◄ The future tense in Gaelic is made by adding the suffix -(a)idh to the end of a verbal noun.

The irregular verb 'to do' 'make' has been used in its future tense form to show how the suffix is applied.

NB The examples here are never used as an auxiliary verb like the other Celtic languages.

Bidh mi	*I will (be)*
Cha bhi mi	*I will not (be)*
Bidh e	*He will (be)*
Cha bhi e	*He will not (be)*
Bidh i	*She will (be)*
Cha bhi i	*She will not (be)*
Bidh ___	*___ will (be)*
Cha bhi ___	*___ will not (be)*

Verbs following the above affix a'/ag before them: **Bidh mi a' bruidhinn** = *I will speak / I will be [at] speaking. No such additions occur when using adjectives.*

b. GNÌOBHAIREAN (*Verbs*)

- Putting **air** before these verbs in Gaelic denotes the perfect tense. The particle **a'** (**ag** before a vowel) are not used with **air** in these cases.
- Much like the other Gaelic languages, some constructions place the verb after the noun. **Bu toil leam sin òl** = *I'd like to drink that* [lit. *I'd like that [to] drink*].

dol (do)	*to go (to)*	**tuigsinn**	*to understand*
faighinn	*to get*	**bruidhinn (ri)**	*to talk, speak (to)*
faighinn	*to have (a)*	**sgrìobhadh**	*to write*
gabhail	*to take*	**leabhagh**	*to read*
còrdadh (ri)	*to enjoy*	**coimhead**	*to watch*
fosgladh	*to open*	**insne (do)**	*to tell (to)*
dùnadh	*to close*	**toirt**	*to give / put*
ithe	*to eat*	**cadal**	*to sleep*
òl	*to drink*	**dèanamh**	*to do*
ceannach	*to buy, purchase*	**bhith**	*to be*
coiseachd	*to walk*	**èisteachd (ri)**	*to listen to*
ruith	*to run*	**smaoineachadh**	*to think*
suidhe	*to sit*	**creideal**	*to believe*
seasamh	*to stand*	**cluinntinn**	*to hear*
caitheamh	*to wear*	**dèidheil (air)**	*to love*
coimhead (air)	*to look (at)*	**ionnsachach**	*to learn*
faicinn	*to see*	**cluich (le)**	*to play (with)*
abair	*to say*	**obair**	*to work*

LÌOMHACHADH (*Lenition*)

B	C	D	F	G	M	P	S	T
BH	CH	DH	FH	GH	MH	PH	SH	TH

Notes on pronunciation & when the **lìomhachadh** happens can be found readily in grammar books etc.

c. BUADHAIREAN (*Adjectives*)

bad	**dona / droch**	*little*	**beag**
beautiful	**brèagha**	*long*	**fada**
big / large	**mòr**	*nasty / evil*	**olc**
boring	**liosta**	*near*	**faisg (air)**
busy	**dripeil / trang**	*new*	**úr**
cheap	**cunnarach / saor**	*next*	**an ath-**
cold	**fuar**	*old*	**sean**
correct	**ceart**	*pretty*	**bòidheach**
dangerous	**cunnartach**	*right (fine, ok)*	**ceart**
different	**diorfar**	*sad*	**duilich**
difficult	**doirbh**	*short*	**geàrr**
dry	**tioram**	*slow*	**mall**
easy / simple	**furasta**	*small*	**beag**
excellent	**iongantach**	*soft*	**maoth**
expensive	**daor**	*special*	**sònraichte**
false / incorrect	**fallsa / mì-cheart**	*sure / certain*	**cinnteach**
fast / quick	**luath**	*tall*	**àrd**
fine	**brèagha / ceart**	*tiny*	**bìodach**
full	**làn**	*tired*	**sgìth**
good	**math**	*true*	**fìor**
happy	**toilichte / sona**	*ugly*	**grànda**
hard	**cruaidh**	*warm*	**blàth**
hot	**teth**	*weak*	**lag**
interesting	**inntinneach**	*wet*	**fliuch**
important	**cudromach**	*young*	**òg**

d. NAISGEARAN (*Conjunctions*)

agus	*and*
ach	*but, however*
no	*or*
a-rithist	*again*
mar sin	*so, therefore*
cuideachd	*too, also*
uaireannan	*sometimes*

e. RIOMHEARAN (*Prepositions*)

mu-dheidhinn	*about*
air	*on*
aig	*at*
le	*with*
gan	*without*
dhan	*to*
airson	*for*
à	*from*
ann	*in*

mi	*me*	**mo** L	*my*
thu	*you*	**do** L	*your*
e	*him*	**a** L	*his*
i	*her*	**a** (+H-)	*her*
sinn	*us*	**ein** (+N-)	*our*
sibh	*you (pl.)*	**(bh)ur** (+N-)	*your (pl.)*
iad	*them*	**an/am**	*their*

LÌOMHACHADH (*Lenition*)

Lenition represents the only initial consonant mutation in Gaelic. There are occasions where **h-**, **n-** and **t-** are added at the beginning of words, as well as inserting 'i' and other letters when dealing with various cases.

f. ABAIRTEAN (*Phrases*)

Maidinn mhath	*Good morning*
Feasgar math	*Good afternoon*
Feasgar math	*Good evening*
Oidhche mhath	*Good night*
Ciamar a tha thu?	*How are you? (Informal)*
Ciamar a tha sibh?	*How are you? (Formal)*
Latha math (dhut / dhuibh)	*Hi / Hello (Inf. / Form.)*
A bheil thu (gu) snog?	*(Are) you alright?*
Slàinte (mhòr)	*Cheers / Good health*
Tìoraidh	*Goodbye*
Mas e do thoil e / Mas e bhur toil e	*Please (Inf. / Form.)*
Tapadh leat / Tapadh leibh	*Thank you (Inf. / Form.)*
Gabh mo leisgeul	*Excuse me*
Tha ____ agam	*I have (got) (a)*
Tha ____ uam	*I want (a / to)*
Feumidh mi	*I need (a / to)*
Chan eil ____ agam	*I don't have*
Chan urrainn mi	*I cannot*
Chan eil mi (e sin) a' tuigsinn	*I don't understand (that)*
Tha mi ag ionnsachadh (na) Gàidhlig	*I'm learning (Scottish) Gaelic*
Alba gu bràth	*Scotland forever*

g. UIBHIREAN (*Numbers*)

Number	Gàidhlig
1	Aon [L]
2	Dà [L] / Dhà [L]
3	Trì
4	Ceithir
5	Còig
6	Sia
7	Seachd
8	Ochd
9	Naoi
10	Deich

h. TEACSA SAMPAILL (*Example text*)

Tha gach uile dhuine air a bhreth saor agus co-ionnan ann an urram 's ann an còirichean. Tha iad air am breth le reusan is le cogais agus mar sin bu chòir dhaibh a bhith beò nam measg fhein ann an spiorad bràthaireil.

All human beings are born free and equal in dignity and rights. They are endowed with reason and conscience and should act towards one another in a spirit of brotherhood.

5. **KERNEWEK** (*Cornish*)

a. AMSERYOW (*Tenses*)

- The particle, **ow**, in Cornish works similarly to the particles '**yn**' and '**o**' in Welsh and Breton respectively in that it expressed that a following verbal noun is in the process of being done or is '*at*' the action. When coupling with adjectives, '**ow**' is dropped.

Yth esov (vy) ow	**... ov**	*I am / do*
Nyns esov ow	**nyns ... ov**	*I am not / I do not*
Yma ev ow	**... yw (ev)**	*He is / He does*
Nyns yw ev ow	**nyns ... yw (ev)**	*He isn't / He doesn't*
Yma hi ow	**... yw (hi)**	*She is / She does*
Nyns yw hi ow	**nyns ... yw (hi)**	*She isn't / She doesn't*
Yma ___ ow	**... yw ___**	*___ is / ___ does*
Nyns yw ___ ow	**nyns ... yw ___**	*___ isn't / ___ doesn't*

Yth esen (vy) ow	*I was*
Nyns esen (vy) ow	*I wasn't*
Yth esa ev ow	*He was*
Nyns esa hi ow	*He wasn't*
Yth esa hi ow	*She was*
Nyns esa hi ow	*She wasn't*
Yth esa ___ ow	*___ was*
Nyns esa ___ ow	*___ wasn't*

> ⚠ *For use with the above - When followed by a verb, the first set of phrases is used. The second set is used when coupling with just nouns and / or adjectives.*

My a wrug	*I did*
Ny wrugav (vy)	*I didn't*
Ev a wrug	*He did*
Ny wrug ev	*He didn't*
Hi a wrug	*She did*
Ny wrug hi	*She didn't*
___ a wrug	*___ did*
Ny wrug ___	*___ didn't*

My a vynsa	*I would like (to)*
Ny vynsa (vy)	*I wouldn't like (to)*
Ev a vynsa	*He would like (to)*
Ny vynsa ev	*He wouldn't like (to)*
Hi a vynsa	*She would like (to)*
Ny vynsa hi	*She wouldn't like (to)*
____ a vynsa	*____ would like (to)*
Ny vynsa ____	*____ wouldn't like (to)*

My a wra / Mynnav	*I will / I wish (to)*
Ny wrav vy / Ny vynnav (vy)	*I won't / I don't wish (to)*
Ev a wra / Mynn ev	*He will / He wishes (to)*
Ny wra ev / Ny vynn (ev)	*He won't / He doesn't wish (to)*
Hi a wra / Mynn hi	*She will / She wishes (to)*
Ny wra hi / Ny vynn (hi)	*She won't / She doesn't wish (to)*
____ a wra / Mynn ____	*____ will / ____ wishes (to)*
Ny wra ____ / Ny vynn ____	*____ won't / ____ doesn't wish (to)*

Bydhav (vy) ow	*I will (be)*
Ny vydhav (vy) ow	*I will not (be)*
Bydh ev ow	*He will (be)*
Ny vydh ev ow	*He will not (be)*
Bydh hi ow	*She will (be)*
Ny vydh hi ow	*She will not (be)*
Bydh ____ ow	*____ will (be)*
Ny vydh ____ ow	*____ will not (be)*

b. VERBOW (*Verbs*)

- The structure 'personal pronoun + **re** + soft mutation (see section at bottom of this page) + verb' in Cornish denotes the perfect tense. The particle **ow** is not used in this case.

mos (dhe)	*to go (to)*	**konvedhes**	*to understand*
kavos[1]	*to get (to)*	**kewsel (gans)**	*to speak, talk (to)*
kavos[2]	*to have (a)*	**skrifa**	*to write*
kemmeres	*to take*	**edya**	*to read*
dotya	*to enjoy*	**golyas**	*to watch*
ygeri	*to open*	**leverel (dhe)**	*to tell (to)*
degea	*to close*	**ri**	*to give / put*
dybri	*to eat*	**hunya, koska**	*to sleep*
eva	*to drink*	**gul**	*to do, make*
prena	*to buy, purchase*	**bos**	*to be*
kerdhes	*to walk*	**goslowes (orth)**	*to listen (to)*
resek	*to run*	**prederi**	*to think*
esedha	*to sit*	**kryji**	*to believe*
sevel	*to stand*	**klywes**	*to hear*
gwiska	*to wear*	**kara**	*to love*
mires (orth)	*to look (at)*	**dyski**	*to learn*
gweles	*to see*	**gwari**	*to play*
leverel (dhe)	*to say (to)*	**ober (rag/yn)**	*to work (for/in)*

AN TREYLYANS MEDHEL (*The Soft Mutation*)

P	T	K	B	D	G[1]	G[2]	GW	M	CH
B	D	G	V	DH	-	W	W	V	J

NB: **G[1]** = before **i, y, e, a, l, ri, ry, re, ra. G[2]** = before **o, u, ro, ru**

c. HENWYN GWANN (*Adjectives*)

- Adjectives (in most cases) follow the noun in Cornish. Just like in Welsh and Breton, a soft mutation occurs with adjectives following feminine nouns (as well as on many other occasions).

bad	**drog**	*interesting*	**didheurek**
beautiful	**teg**	*important*	**posek**
big, large	**meur**	*little*	**byghan**
boring	**skwithus**	*long*	**hir**
busy	**bysi**	*mean, nasty*	**anhwek, asper**
cheap	**a bris isel**	*near, close*	**nes, ogas**
cold	**oer**	*new*	**nowydh**
correct	**gwir, ewn**	*next*	**nessa**
dangerous	**peryllus**	*old*	**koth**
different	**dyffrans**	*pretty*	**kader, teg**
difficult	**kales**	*right (okay)*	**gwir**
dry	**sygh**	*sad*	**trist**
easy, simple	**es, sempl**	*short*	**berr**
excellent	**splann**	*slow*	**lent**
expensive	**kostek**	*small*	**byghan**
false	**fals**	*soft*	**medhel**
fast, quick	**uskis, buan**	*special*	**arbennik**
fine	**brav**	*sure, certain*	**kowgans, sur**
full	**leun**	*tall*	**hir**
good	**da**	*tired*	**skwith**
happy	**lowen**	*true*	**gwir**
hard	**kales**	*ugly*	**hager**
hot	**poeth**	*wet*	**glyb**
incorrect	**anewn**	*young*	**yowynk**

d. GERYOW KEVRENN (*Conjunctions*)

ha (hag before a vowel)	*and*
mes	*but / however*
po	*or*
hwath	*yet*
arta	*again*
ytho	*so*
ynwedh	*too / also*
treweythyo	*sometimes*

e. RAGERYOW (*Prepositions*)

a-dro (dhe)	*about*
war	*on*
war-tu	*towards*
gans	*by / with*
heb	*without*
dhe	*to / for / at*
a	*of / from*
yn / y'n	*in / in the*

HWITHYS AM
(*Aspirate Mutation*)

P	F
T	TH
K	H

KALES HM
(*Hard Mutation*)

B	P
D	T
G	K

my, vy	*me*	**ow** AM	*my*
ty	*you*	**dha** SM	*your*
ev	*him*	**y** SM	*his*
hi	*her*	**hy** AM	*her*
ni	*us*	**(a)gan**	*our*
hwi	*you (pl.)*	**(ag)as**	*your (pl.)*
i	*them*	**(a)ga** AM	*their*

SM = Soft Mutation

AM = Aspirate Mutation

HM = Hard Mutation

(Found on verbs following

the particle '**ow**' et al)

f. LAVAROW (*Phrases*)

Myttin da	*Good morning*
Dohajydh da	*Good afternoon*
Gorthugher da	*Good evening*
Nos da	*Good night*
Fatla genes?	*How are you? (Informal)*
Fatla genowgh (hwi)?	*How are you? (Formal)*
Hou / Ha	*Hi*
Poynt da?	*(Are) you alright?*
Yeghes da	*Cheers / Good health*
Dew genes / Dha weles	*Goodbye*
Mar pleg	*Please*
Meur ras	*Thank you*
Gav dhymm	*Excuse me*

_____ (yw) genev	*I have (got) (a)*
My a vynn	*I want (a / to)*
Res yw dhymm (kavos)	*I need (to) (have (a))*
Nyns _____ yw genev	*I don't have*
Ny allav (vy)	*I am failing / I cannot*
Ny gonvedhav (henna)	*I don't understand (that)*
Yth esov ow tyski <u>Kernewek</u>	*I'm learning <u>Cornish</u>*

<u>Kernow</u> bys vyken	*<u>Cornwall</u> forever*

g. NIVEROW (*Numbers*)

Number	Kernewek *Masc. / Fem.*
1	**Unn / Unn** SM (& Onan is used when counting items)
2	**Dew** SM **/ Diw** SM
3	**Tri** AM **/ Teir** AM
4	**Peswar / Peder**
5	**Pymp**
6	**Hwegh**
7	**Seyth**
8	**Eth**
9	**Naw**
10	**Deg**

h. TEKST SEMPEL (*Example Text*)

Pub den oll yw genys rydh hag kehaval yn dynita ha gwiryow. Yth yns i kemynnys gans reson ha kowses hag y tal dhedha gul dhe unn orth y gila yn spyrys a vrederedh.

All human beings are born free and equal in dignity and rights. They are endowed with reason and conscience and should act towards one another in a spirit of brotherhood.

6. **BREZHONEG** (*Breton*)

a. AMZEROÙ (*Tenses* / *Les Temps*)

Emaon o	**... on**	*I am / do*	Je [suis]
N'emaon ket o	**n'on ket**	*I am not / I do not*	Je ne [suis] pas
Emañ o	**... eo (ev)**	*He / He is / He does*	Il [est]
N'emañ ket o	**n'eo ket**	*He isn't / He doesn't*	Il ne [est] pas
Emañ (hi) o	**... eo (hi)**	*She / She is / She does*	Elle [est]
N'emañ (hi) ket o	**n'eo ket**	*She isn't / She doesn't*	Elle ne [est] pas
Emañ ___ o	**... eo**	*___ is / ___ does*	___ [est]
N'emañ ___ ket o	**n'eo ket**	*___ isn't / ___ doesn't*	___ ne [est] pas

Me a oa	**... am eus**	*I was*	J'etais
Ne a oan	**... n'am eus ket**	*I wasn't*	Je n'etais pas
Eñ a oa	**... e deus**	*He was*	Il etait
Ne oa ket	**n'e deus ket**	*He wasn't*	Il n'etait pas
Hi a oa	**... he deus**	*She was*	Elle etait
Ne oa ket	**n'he deus ket**	*She wasn't*	Elle n'etait pas
___ a oa	**... en deus**	*___ was*	___ etait
___ ne oa ket	**___ n'e deus ket**	*___ wasn't*	___ n'etait pas

> ⚠ *When using the above followed by a verb, the first set of phrases is used. The second set is used when coupling with just nouns and/or adjectives.*

... a raen	*I did*	J'ai [été]
Ne raen ket	*I didn't*	Je n'ai [été] ... pas
... a rea	*He did*	Il a [été]
Ne rea ket	*He didn't*	Il n'a [été] ... pas
... a rea	*She did*	Elle a [été]
Ne rea ket	*She didn't*	Elle n'a [été] ... pas
... a rea ___	*___ did*	___ a [été]
Ne rea ket ___	*___ didn't*	___ n'a [été] ... pas

Plijout a rafe din	*I would like (to)*	Je voudrais
Ne rafe blij ket din	*I wouldn't like (to)*	Je ne voudrais pas
Plijout a rafe dezhañ	*He would like (to)*	Il voudrait
Ne rafe blij ket dezhañ	*He wouldn't like (to)*	Il ne voudrait pas
Plijout a rafe dezhi	*She would like (to)*	Elle voudrait
Ne rafe blij ket dezhañ	*She wouldn't like (to)*	Elle ne voudrait pas
Plijout a rafe da ___	*___ would like (to)*	___ voudrait
Ne rafe blik ket da ___	*___ wouldn't like (to)*	___ ne voudrait pas

Me a ra	*I will*	Je vais
Ne ran ket	*I won't*	Je ne vais pas
Eñ a ra	*He will*	Il va
Ne ra ket	*He won't*	Il ne va pas
Hi a ra	*She will*	Elle va
Ne ra ket	*She won't*	Elle ne va pas
___ a ra	*___ will*	___ va
Ne ra ___ ket	*___ won't*	___ ne va pas

Me a vo	**... a rin**	*I will (be)*	Je [se]rai
Ne vezan ket	**ne rin ket**	*I will not (be)*	Je ne [se]rai
Eñ a vo	**... a raio**	*He will (be)*	Il [se]ra
Ne vo ket	**ne raio ket**	*He will not (be)*	Il ne [se]ra pas
Hi a vo	**... a raio**	*She will (be)*	Elle [se]ra
Ne vo ket	**ne raio ket**	*She will not (be)*	Elle ne [se]ra pas
___ a vo	**... a raio ___**	*___ will (be)*	___ [se]ra
Ne vo ___ ket	**ne raio ___ ket**	*___ will not (be)*	___ ne [se]ra pas

b. VERBOÙ (*Verbs* / Les Verbes)

mont (da)	*to go to*	aller	**gompren**	*to understand*	comprendre
kaout	*to get*	avoir	**skrivañ**	*to write*	ecrire
rankout	*to have (a)*	avoir	**lenn**	*to read*	lire
kemer	*to take*	prendre	**diwall**	*to watch*	regarder
bourrañ	*to enjoy*	aimer	**lavaret**	*to tell*	dire
digeriñ	*to open*	ouvre	**komz**	*to speak, talk*	parler
klozañ	*to close*	fermer	**reiñ, lakaat**	*to give, put*	donner
debriñ	*to eat*	manger	**kousket**	*to sleep*	dormir
evañ	*to drink*	boire	**ober**	*to do, make*	faire
prenañ	*to buy*	acheter	**bezañ**	*to be*	être
kerzhet	*to walk*	marcher	**klevet**	*to listen*	ecoûter
redek	*to run*	courir	**soñjal**	*to think*	penser
azezañ	*to sit*	asseoir	**krediñ**	*to believe*	croire
sevel	*to stand*	tenir	**klevet**	*to hear*	entendre
gwiskañ	*to wear*	porter	**karout**	*to love*	aimer
sell(et)	*to look*	regarder	**deskiñ**	*to learn*	apprendre
gwelet	*to see*	voir	**c'hoari**	*to play*	jouer
lavaret	*to say*	dire	**labour**	*to work*	travailler

c. ANVIOÙ-GWAN (*Adjectives* / Les Adjectifs masculines)

English	Breton	French	English	Breton	French
bad	drouk, fall	mauvais	incorrect	direizh	incorrect
beautiful	brav, kaer	beau	interesting	dedennus	interesant
big, tall	bras	grand	important	pouezus	important
boring	enoeüs	ennuyeux	little, small	bihan	petit
busy	a'chub	occupé	long	hir, pell	long
cheap	marc'had-mat	pas cher	nasty, evil	drouk	mauvais
cold	yen	froid	near	e-kichen	à côte de
correct	reizh	correct	new	nevez	nouveau
dangerous	dañjerus	dangereux	next	kentañ	prochain
different	dishañval	différent	old	kozh	vieux
difficult	diaes	difficile	pretty	koant	joli
dry	sec'h	sec	right (honest)	eeun	honest
easy, simple	aes	facil	sad	trist	trist
excellent	dispar	excellent	short	berr	court
expensive	daor	cher	slow	gorrek	lent
false, wrong	mícheart	faux	soft	dous(ik)	doux
fast, quick	buan	rapid	special	ispicial	spécial
fine	brav	d'accord	sure / certain	sur	sûrement
full	leun, leizh	plein	tired	skuizh	fatigué
good	mat	bon	true	gwir	vrai
happy	laouen	content	ugly	divalav, vil	laid
hard	kalet	dur	wet	gleb	de pluie
hot	te	chaud	young	yaouank	jeun

AR C'HEMMADURIOÙ DRE VLOTAAT (*The Soft Mutation* / La Lénition)

P	T	K	B	D	G	GW	M
B	D	G	V	Z	C'H	W	V

d. STAGELLOÙ (*Conjunctions* / Les Conjonctions)

ha (hag + vowel / voyelle)	*and*	et
met	*but / however*	mais
pe	*or*	ou
adarre	*again*	encore
evel-se	*so*	donc
ivez	*too, also*	aussi
a-wechoù, a-wezhioù	*sometimes*	parfois

e. ARAOGENNOÙ (*Prepositions* / Les Prépositions)

diwar-benn	*about*	pour, environ
war [SM]	*on*	sur
war-du	*towards*	vers
gant / dre	*with / by*	avec
hep	*without*	sans
da [SM]**, evid**	*to / for / at*	à, pour
eus, a	*of / from*	de
e / en	*in / in the*	dans / dans le/la

me	*me*	moi	**ma** [AM] *my*	ma, mon, mes
te	*you*	toi	**da** [SM] *your*	ta, ton, tes
eñ	*him*	il	**e** [SM] *his*	sa, son, ses
hi	*her*	elle	**he**[1][AM] *her*	sa, son, ses
ni	*we*	nous	**hol**[2] *our*	notre, nos
c'hwi	*you*	vous	**ho**[3][HM] *your*	votre, vos
i	*them*	ils, elles	**o** [AM] *their*	leur(s)

[1] **hec'h** before vowel [2] also **hon, hor** [3] **hoc'h** before vowel

C'HWEZHADENNIÑ [AM] (*Aspirate Mutation*)

P	F
T	Z
K	C'H

KALET [HM] (*Hard Mutation*)

B	P
D	T
G	K

f. RANNFRAZENNOÙ (*Phrases*) (Les Phrases)

Devezh mat	*Good morning*	Bon matin
Endervezh vat	*Good afternoon*	Bon après-midi
Nozvezh vat	*Good evening*	Bonsoir
Noz vat	*Good night*	Bonne nuit
Mat an traoù?	*How are you?*	(Comment) ça va?
Demat	*Hi / Hello*	Bonjour
Mont a ra?	*(Are) you alright?*	Ça va?
Yec'hed mat	*Cheers / Good health*	(Bonne) santé
Kenavo	*Goodbye*	Au revoir
Mar plij (deoc'h)	*Please*	S'il vous plaît
Trugarez	*Thank you*	Merci (beaucoup)
Digarez	*Excuse me*	Excusez moi

___ zo ganin	*I have (got) (a)*	J'ai (un / une)
C'hoant am eus	*I want (a / to)*	Je veux (un / une)
Ret eo din	*I need (to)*	Je besoin (un / une)
N'eus ___ ebet ganin	*I don't have*	Je n'ai pas (un / une)
N'hellan ket	*I cannot*	Je ne peux pas
Ne gomprenan ket	*I don't understand*	Je ne comprends pas
Me a ra deskiñ <u>brezhoneg</u>	*I'm learning <u>Breton</u>*	J'apprends le <u>breton</u>
Me a zesk <u>brezhoneg</u>		

<u>Breizh</u> atao	*<u>Brittany</u> forever*	<u>Bretagne</u> toujours

g. NIVERENNOÙ (*Numbers* / Les Nombres)

Number *Nombre*	Brezhoneg *Masc. / Fem.*	Français
1	**Unan**	Un(e)
2	**Daou** [SM] **/ Div** [SM]	Deux
3	**Tri** [AM] **/ Teir** [AM]	Trois
4	**Pevar** [AM] **/ Peder** [AM]	Quatre
5	**Pemp**	Cinq
6	**C'hwec'h**	Six
7	**Seizh**	Sept
8	**Eizh**	Huit
9	**Nav** [AM]	Neuf
10	**Dek**	Dix

h. TESTEN SKOUER (*Example Text* / Exemple de Texte)

Dieub ha par en o dellezegezh hag o gwirioù eo ganet an holl dud. Poell ha skiant zo dezho ha dleout a reont bevañ an eil gant egile en ur spered a genvreudeuriezh.

All human beings are born free and equal in dignity and rights. They are endowed with reason and conscience and should act towards one another in a spirit of brotherhood.

Tous les êtres humains naissent libres et égaux en dignité et en droits. Ils sont doués de raison et de conscience et doivent agir les uns envers les autres dans un esprit de fraternité.

THE (definite article) le, la, les, l' (l'article défini)	Singular / Le Singulier				Plural / Le Pluriel			
	C - C	C - V	V - C	V - V	C - C	C - V	V - C	V - V
Cymraeg	y	yr	'r	'r	y	yr	'r	'r
Gaeilge	an	an	an	an	na	na^{+H}	na	na^{+H}
Gaelg	yn, 'n, y	yn, 'n, y	yn, 'n, y	yn, 'n, y	ny	ny	ny	ny
Gàidhlig	a', am an (t-)	a', am an (t-)	a', am an (t-)	a', am an (t-)	na, nan, nam	na (h-), nan	na, nan, nam	na (h-), nan
Kernewek	an	an	'n	'n	an	an	'n	'n
Brezhoneg	an, ar, al	an, ar, al	an, ar, al	an, ar, al	an, ar, al	an, ar, al	an, ar, al	an, ar, al

C – C =   Final letter of preceeding word is a consonant

First letter of following word is a consonant

C – V =   Final letter of preceeding word is a consonant

First letter of following word is a vowel

V – C =   Final letter of preceeding word is a vowel

First letter of following word is a consonant

V – V =   Final letter of preceeding word is a vowel

First letter of following word is a vowel

In all Celtic languages, feminine singular nouns receive a mutation after the definite article. These are explained in more detail in each language's respective section.

YMARFERION / CLÀR-INNSE / CUMMAL / CLÁR ÁBHAIR / SYNSAS / DONVEZIOÙ
(*Exercises*) (Les Teneurs)

Try to translate these yourself:
Remember, this book does not contain nouns. You will need to look these up in dictionaries or by using online lexicons.

1. I am learning Welsh
2. He is not making a large cake
3. She loves her cat too
4. Owen is not reading the correct book
5. I'd like to eat again
6. I was learning Welsh
7. He was not making a large cake
8. She was loving her cat too
9. Owen was not reading the correct book
10. She'd like to eat again

GWEFANNAU / LÀRAICH-LÌN / YNNYDYN EGGEY / GRÉASÁIN / GWIASVAOW / LEC'HIENNOÙ
(*Websites*) (Sites d'Internet)

Cymraeg: SSIW / Duolingo / Omniglot / ClozeMaster / DysguCymraeg.cymru

Gaeilge: Duolingo / Omniglot / ClozeMaster / Gaelchultur.com

Gàidhlig: Duolingo / Omniglot / LearnGaelic.net

Gaelg: Omniglot / Culture Vannin / SSIW / LearnManx.com

Kernewek: Radyo an Gernewegva / LearnCornish.org
/ Clozemaster / Omniglot / SSIW
Brezhoneg: Omniglot / ClozeMaster / MissionBretonne.bzh

NODIADAU / NÓTAÍ / SCREEUYN / NOTAICHEAN / NOTYANSOW / NOTENNOÙ

(*Notes*) (Les Annotations)

NODIADAU / NÓTAÍ / SCREEUYN / NOTAICHEAN / NOTYANSOW / NOTENNOÙ
(*Notes*) (Les Annotations)

NODIADAU / NÓTAÍ / SCREEUYN / NOTAICHEAN / NOTYANSOW / NOTENNOÙ
(*Notes*) (Les Annotations)

**NODIADAU / NÓTAÍ / SCREEUYN /
NOTAICHEAN / NOTYANSOW / NOTENNOÙ**
(*Notes*) (Les Annotations)

**NODIADAU / NÓTAÍ / SCREEUYN /
NOTAICHEAN / NOTYANSOW / NOTENNOÙ**
(*Notes*) (Les Annotations)

Printed in Great Britain
by Amazon